THE DONNY DIARIES

HOW A NOT SO DONNY PRESIDENT PROCESSES HIS DONNY DAYS

-

POLITICAL SATIRE 4 DONNY FANS & FAKEFAN #DONNY DETRACTORS

BY CALLUM COKER

"The last time I was on this stage I was 6, I was...

Miley. And I still am".

Miley Cyrus

ISBN 978-1-991338-49-5

Paperback.

First International Trade edition: November 2024.

A CIP catalogue record for this book is available from the National Library of New Zealand.

OTHER BOOKS BY CALLUM COKER

THE FREEDOM MESSAGE: PSALMS

THE FREEDOM MESSAGE: PROVERBS

THE FREEDOM MESSAGE: ECCLESIASTES

THE FREEDOM MESSAGE: GALATIANS

THE FREEDOM MESSAGE: EPHESIANS

THE FREEDOM MESSAGE: PHILIPPIANS

THE FREEDOM MESSAGE: GALATIANS +

FREEDOM POINTS

THE FREEDOM MESSAGE: PSALMS LARGE

PRINT EDITION

THE FREEDOM MESSAGE: PROVERBS LARGE

PRINT EDITION

DISCLAIMER

This book is entirely fiction. No Donny diary entry is factual. The characters are fake personas and designed for the purposes of satire and humour. If you don't laugh that's your choice or better jokes need to be doth written. No donny's were harmed or intended to be harmed in the making of this not so donny diary.

DISCLAIMER

This book is a work of fiction. No [illegible] any thing [illegible] story is factual. The characters are false persona[illegible] and designed for the purposes of [illegible] and humour. If [illegible] that's [illegible] better [illegible] the [illegible] [illegible] enough to [illegible] [illegible] [illegible]

DEAR DONNY DIARY

THIS IS DONNYS DIARY I'VE GOT MY MCDONALD CHIPS NEXT TO ME THAT I GET A MAID TO CROSS OFF THE Mc part in Mc BONALD'S cos I'm top Donald no other Donald in the history of Mcdonald's can compete with this Donald. To be in the donny diaries u have to be the best Donald and that won't fly with me. Uuuuuuuuuuuure fired! mCdonald's now new Donald's fries that aren't even half cooked now that I'm in charge of the country since I bet that ole vintage lady who would of maybe made it into one of my beauty pageants back in the day kamaaaallaaa, donny would have probably been dating her if she wasn't my daughter I mean running mate, I mean ummm hmmm political opponent. Stay cool Donald stay very cool now ole donny boy I've seen the ole kamala pics wen she was a honey but she's not a honey now she's a meany to real life current Donald @notsorealdonald trump 4 real now. I need to find more votes for this new venture of Donald's to compete with the Og Mcdonald's y am I even in politics I should be nicking their real estate taking their staff and then firing them all and turning the mcdonald's stores into beautiful high rise buildings with TRUMP at the top of them that's wat Donald does he outdoes the DONNY all day the only person who can compete with this Donald is my Donald which entirely belongs to me so shame on u false DONNY impersonado's! is that even a word?! Do I even care, do I even check my spelling?! Its my diary I'm the boss of this operation, u want operation Donald u got operation Donald. Now lets say a prayer for all those kamala voters. Republicans love Jesus and I'm a republican now and to get republican votes I need Jesus! So dear Jesus make Donald great again by making America gr8 again u make Donald gr8 again and I like ole donny boy gr8!!!! See how many xclamation marks I doth jus used home boy ole boy-o that's was a lot!!!! Oh and ahh Amen?! That was donny diaries bliss that donny sentence, only a true Donald could make a donny exclamation mark like that no other exclamation marks were needed I used just the rite amount to be a truthful Donald. Thanks for reading my diary Donald, I typed – I soliloqued it and I donald't it that's rite Donald won this diary entry onto the next home boy top dawg donny!

3

DEAR DONNY DIARY 2

People often ask me: How do I Donald? wen there are no other donald's like me, no one can Donald like me not even Donald duck from walt Disney or walt watever his last name is or the impersonator donald's they are fake donalds! I don't like fake news media just as much as I don't like fake donald's they are the worst kind of donald's those donald's they are not worthy of Donald chips or Donald dips that's rite I change my dips 2 that's wat Donald does, who needs a spell checker wen I am the spell checker I'm the fact checker the model checker the check checker and the bozo democratic nominee out ya go cos donald's here checker. All those checkpoints have a Donald attached to them if u want a real life @notsorealdonald trump to help u navigate ur not so donny days I'll send one to you it will just cost u a buck fifty adjusted to inflation that rounds out to around.... 600 million smackers not dollars smackers ive renamed cash b4 but I think its appropriate that I give it a new name a name befitting of the top Donald that I am, there we go I've renamed it again no longer is it pingaz or cash or moolah or smackerz its donny dollars, just think the USD ends with a donny letter, that's the first part of the mcdonald trump name, I choosie that all us citizens are now 2 b named Donald citizens except for the illegal aliens get McDonald dollars these dollars r the bestest kind of dollars far superior to Mongolian dollars or the kiwi yen who da faaaak@ wants to go visit New Zealand?! THEY DO HAVE NICE GOLF COURSES THOUGH AND MOUNTAINS AND LAKES AND RIVERS AND MONEY AND DONNYFANS LOTS AND LOTS OF DONNY FANS AND JOHN KEY WHO IS OFCOURSE A DONNY FAN! #ILIKEDONNYFANS! any ways u can just come to the architect pad of the world palace my honeybun New York city baby lots of cash and that's where I store safely my Melania she belongs to me! I paid for her to be my third wife or is it my fourth I don't know I don't care she's hawt and that's all that counts once she's not hawt I can trade her in for a younger melania leo dicaprio style, but we aren't talking about leo in this donny diary entry again that's not okay he's a democrat boooooooooyakashah!!! The democrats even false ones with Italian names who like fake models 4 missuses just like me

Donald the @notsorealdonald trump don't get ne tweets from mehomeboy.

@realdonnymabebsofakesodonnydiaryboi-boi-0!

@#tweeetme

@nadonttweetmereadthenextdonnyentryinsteadorwatchadonnyyoutubevideoorhavearealdonaldchiporsomething!

#donnychipsrstillinfashion

#donnyfashion

#THErestofthePAGEBELOWEXAMINESKAMALAHARISSESLIFETIMEACHIEVEMENTS…

DEAR DONNY DIARY 3

#UTHOUGHTUWEREGONAGETADONNYDIARYENTRY

3UTHOUGHTWRONG

@UCANGETACODEDMESSAGEVIADONNYCODEINSTEADCOSTHATSWATDONNYDOESHEKEEPSUGUESSINGTHEDONNYMEDIAFOXNEWSGUESSINGANDTHEFAKENEWSCIHAVNTEVENTURNEDOFFMYCAPSLOCK BRB OR NAAA!

#LETsRETURNTOAHASHTAGSHALLWEORSHAN'TWE?@!

ITSMOREADONNYPOEMTHISSECTIONOFMYDIARYOFTHEBESTESTDONNY

THIS ISLIKEMYPICASSOITWONTMAKESENSETOMANYITSABSTRACTARTOFDONNYWITHMYUNDONNYLAPTOP

@#

WATDOESTHEHASHTAGEVENMEANNEWAYIFITDOESNTHAVEADONALDNEXTTOIT?!

7

#KNOWDONALDNOWAYISITGONNABEADONNY

#@!WHeresmymcdoladtrumpmaidgone?!

#whreshebatmikepencemikegetouttahereuwantedmyjobnowurfiredeventhoutriedtofireme

#baddymike

#isthishowuusehashtags?!

#?

DEAR DONNY DIARY QUATRE

People often say to me y did u name ur Donald diary quatre – quatre rather than donny diary 4 like a usual Donald and I just say to them it's simple I met masseur macron today, c there I go again speaking french or is it Spanish or is some other donny combination of the two languages that wud make my French and Spanish teacher blush because she was in the presence of young 13 year old Donald knowing that future Donald would be president of the united states of cos donald's in the white house so u shud jus stay united rather than try to make fake civil wars and fake media wars with fake media channels. I've blocked off all fake media channels and jus listen to truth social cos if I say it it must be true. Donald doesn't lie see that statement was true I mite tweet that or truth social that, I love truth social all other socials aren't true that's why there is a media now called donald media owned by donald. But notice how I'v3 been getting chummy with ole Elon Musk?! I was think me donny and I and Elon and whats his face ole JD

Vance could be called the three 'Musk'eteers but that wouldn't be fair on the Donald and although Elon's not as smart as me or have as much Real Estate dollars as me I mean the dude doesn't even live in a white house he lives in a shack that Tesla built I'm pretty sure?! Didn't they jus do rockets or cars or sumthing of that ilk? I don't know, all I know is if we are gonna b and stay pals he needs to know that I'm FAR-FAR-FAR more genius than him and richer and got way hotter exes and future missuses or wives or whatever arrangement that works for my love twosies that I choosie.

Now back to masseur macaroni or macron that's his nickname I'm pretty sure masseur de'la veiagga macron delamucci he has a bit of Greek im pretty sure so im not sure if I am sure but all I know is that wat I say is true #truth social #truthdonald tells the truth all the truth and so help me Donald dear apprecianado's!

DEAR DONNY DIARY 5

I WANT 2 TALKTODAY ABOUT DONNY SELECTION POLICIES! Did that feel like I was yelling? That really wasn't the donny tone I was after, a happy Donald makes for a peaceful Donald and the more peace there is in the world of the Donald the happier Donald hippos and lamas will be, I don't have a hippo or a lama pet but I do have JD Vance, wat a legendary pick that was, my son Donald trump jnr made that one like a true jnr Donald, did I call him Donald Trump Jnr? That's what I wish his name was 4 realZ! Dawg, that or Snoop Dogg but snoops name was actually taken and that made for an unhappy Donald. When I select my team I have three questions that I routinely check they are donny greenlights kinda like the Matthew Mconaughey book I think it was a good book that book, I didn't actually read the book but I read the title and I thought 'that's catchy that's cool' #kewlmattypatatty

= more moolah4matty!

Now back to my donny selections, the key to a good Donald trump staffer is:

1. b loyal to the don.

2. Stay loyal to the don.

3. Let the Donald speak wen spoken too always call DJT 45TH AND 47TH King Donald of USA.

4 If we golf I win and I set the scores per hole of the win. More Donald wins means less Donald losses.

5. Call Eric Donald trump jnr eric, I wanted his middle name to be shin but one of my first or second wives wudnt let me call him that so I jus call him the Donald lil guy in my diary ofcourse.

6. Make sure if there are females around me they are smokin' hawt no rosie o'donnells allowed #EVER!

7. You need to not speak mexican in my vicinity, Mexicans are bringing crime like I do It's just they are more Mexican than me so it's not okay.

8. u need to let me win in a tug of war challenge thumb war challenge, noughts and crosses challenge, biblical trivia challenge and USA president election challenge.

9 u need to have a fav verse of the Bible cos I don't have one, just to know the Bible and attach my name to it with Trump Bible is okily dockily by me.

10. U need to write me a 'I love donny cos' poem once every quatre cos well dats jus how I b ya know..?! ya dig.

11. Discard all of these steps if I meet ya, I like ya and ur donny approved, donny hired and lil donny jnr likes ya cos I like lil donny jnr, if he was nt my son I'd probs still hire him cos he kinda looks like me a lil bit and wife number two or one whichever one is his mum, I like the lad.

#ladtastic.

13

DEAR DONNY DIARY 6

Today I want to talk about Ivanka dearest diary of diaryness #diaryville #diaryessa. I miss Ivanka I flicked her a txt and a truth social message that my truth social data person wouldn't let me tweet or non tweet or truth out there to the world of truth social. She jus was like 'truth social isn't meant for Ivanka it's meant for fellow truthers, people who love the truth so help them Donald.' So I flicked Ivanka a txt and it said 'sup ivanka best daughter more bester than tiff, how's things? Been on a talk show recently with Joe Rogan it went on for ages I could have made so much money in that time but I actually just made money for Joe, Joes got the cash but I'm hoping that I get the votes, if I get the votes I win and if I don't get the votes I claim I get the votes and then win that way but don't win its technically not a win but I make it a win. C u next Wednesday for a talk show like we did years back? It would be like our very own Father daughter time ya know? Ivanka dearest ur presence in my 1st election run was crucial to

Donald victory so Donald wants Ivanka back for a unanimous Donald victory parade celebrations. Let's change the subject shall we. How's things at home? Did u get those chickens I sent u? Kentucky fried chickens that is? They are the awesomest kind of chickens. I had a bucket last week, JD chomped on a few of them and then handed them over I wasn't unimpressed but I was definitely more than slightly surprised. Anyway, glad u got this message I miss u but not too much cos Donald doesn't miss anybody he just soldiers on forward into the next donny project. So if I don't c u b4 xmas in the words of bartholomews erectus, b*witched and moonshineshadow46@livespace@hotmail.com

'ce'st la vie'

DEAR DONNY DIARY 7

It's election night round three and I wouldn't know what to do if it wasn't for the previous two fight nights for emperor of USA that I went through. I won the first one fair and square from Hilz #getaprosecutorasap4datlady and JB #yuhavetonotretireandjustletmewin?! And the third one kammy @kammyonceuponatimewashawtness. I miss Hilz a bit I wonder if she asks after me over a nice seafood dinner with billy saying 'hey billy wonder what's donny upto? Do u think he would like to play Bingo with me next Friday night after a gelato, we could maybe play some Backgammon. I think Donny would let me win at Backgammon. Not much else though he wouldn't let us have our old White House back the same White House Channing tatum rescued in a film about our old residence. We got that pad for 4 WHOLE American years with no rent money, that was AWESOME it was so AWESOME, I gave it a nudge to get the keys back off Barack, I miss Donny though, can we just remember the good ole boi donny days for just a moment when we were the bestest buddies in the whole wide world of America?! Be a good billy not a bad billy thanks shugar.' Well this has been rad, I'm off tomorrow to go catch up with my old pal Mike Pence, na I'm jus jokin' that would be far to scandalous like me in a backgammon match with Hilz.

17

DEAR DONNY DIARY 8

We are coming to the end of our donny diaries now. Y so? I hear u say well quite simply a donny like this has a youtube channel to think of and take care of a nation while I play golf and there's no democrats close by, what is more scary to the United States people? Donald Trump or the democrat? Clearly it was me baybee! that's why I've been picked as President three times in succession that's better than the crem de la crem of trilogies better than the Hangover trilogy and the Lord of the Rings trilogy that ironically didn't have that many scenes with medieval bling in it tbh, they have got to add more bling. The key to winning the presidency is be me that's it, final, no questions asked no way am I sharing any other clues and/or tips on how to get the me deal done for the American people, I make great deals the best deals in the history of deals. No one makes deals like Alpha donny! The rogue deals of old would only long for a deal like the donny political career that I've forged with alot of Jesus, hillbillies and Mexican supporters. That's right I boot out those mexicano's 4 sure! But If they stay legally they can vote for me that's been my strategy since the first day and it's working well I leave the good hombres here in Mexican cities of the united States and I give them Trumpy cred for doing so. I've seen some good diaries in my time but no diary is quite like this one this is the best diary u will read in the history of diaries now it's time to give Melania a call she wants me to tell her that I'm the best husband since Mcdonald's was invented and now I must say

Adieu!

FIN

ABOUT THE AUTHOR

Callum Coker is an author of over 20 books including his groundbreaking work THE FREEDOM MESSAGE that reimagines the world of the Bible within the context of the 21st Century, his interests include, reading, poetry, sport and Sanna Marin.

www.ingramcontent.com/pod-product-compliance
Lightning Source LLC
LaVergne TN
LVHW020544160826
845677LV00015B/4199

* 9 7 8 1 9 9 1 3 3 8 4 9 5 *